SCHOLASTIC
Let's Find Out
My REBUS Reader

I See Seeds!

by Joan Michael

SCHOLASTIC INC.
New York Toronto London Auckland Sydney New Delhi Hong Kong

I see seeds. They are in a 

.

I see seeds. They are in a  .

pod

I see seeds. They are in a  .

watermelon

I see seeds. They are in a .

pumpkin

I see seeds. They are in a  .

birdfeeder

I see a seed. It is in a .

peach

Count the Seeds

Which fruit has the most?

orange

apple

cucumber

lemon